THE HOLY SPIRIT

A

Scripture for Meditation: 9

THE HOLY SPIRIT

Henry Wansbrough OSB

St Paul Publications

ST PAUL PUBLICATIONS
SLOUGH   SL3 6BT   ENGLAND

Nihil obstat: Gerard E. Roberts, Censor
Imprimatur: + Charles Grant, Bishop of Northampton
14 May 1973

Printed in Great Britain by the Society of St Paul, Slough

SBN 85439 094 4

CONTENTS

BIBLE PASSAGES USED

OLD TESTAMENT

NEW TESTAMENT

ACKNOWLEDGEMENT

The Bible text in this publication is from the Revised Standard Version Bible, Catholic Edition, copyrighted © 1965 and 1966 by the Division of Christian Education of the National Council of the Churches of Christ in the U.S.A., and used by permission.

FOREWORD

The revelation of the third Person of the Trinity was a gradual process. In the Old Testament there was at first no realization even that he existed; though from the earliest times the Bible spoke of the Spirit of God, this was conceived only as God active in the world, not as a separate power, let alone a personal one. It was only after many centuries that concentration on the intellectual aspect of Wisdom brought near the realization of a Person distinguishable from the Creator but united to him and sharing in his activities and powers. The revelation in the New Testament of the Paraclete who is to come to the Church to fill the place of Jesus after his departure, and of the Spirit which fills Christians and works as their life-force, then led on to the fuller doctrine of the holy Spirit.

There is, then, a rich and varied development in the Bible which enables us to appreciate the many aspects of the Spirit. The Spirit is the life-force of Christians, and is as many-sided as life, active in countless ways and at many different levels. Only the Spirit can enable the Christian to learn more and more to appreciate and be filled by the Spirit.

HENRY WANSBROUGH

Ampleforth Abbey
April 1973

1

THE SPIRIT BLOWS WHERE IT WILLS

Genesis 1:1- 2

In the beginning God created the heavens and the earth. The earth was without form and void, and darkness was upon the face of the deep; and the Spirit of God was moving over the face of the waters.

John 3:5-8

Truly, truly, I say to you, unless one is born of water and the Spirit, he cannot enter the kingdom of God. That which is born of the flesh is flesh, and that which is born of the Spirit is spirit. Do not marvel that I said to you, 'You must be born anew.' The wind blows where it wills, and you hear the sound of it, but you do not know whence it comes or whither it goes; so it is with every one who is born of the Spirit.

Reflection

Beginnings are always mysterious and fascinating, especially when they contain the germ, as yet unrecognized, of great things. At the beginning of the Bible comes this mysterious passage, full of presage for the unknown future. The Hebrew did not think of nothingness as void but as formlessness: in the beginning nothing existed because what there was was no thing, like a picture thrown on a screen totally out of focus and so a picture of nothing. But waiting to bring being out of nothingness was the power of the Spirit of God, hovering over the waters — a superb image of creative power as yet unrealized.

There are so many aspects of the Spirit that it is impossible to exhaust all ways of looking at it, but perhaps the one to start with is this all-potency of God. It is the Spirit which transforms chaos into meaningfulness. In the book of Genesis this is represented as a temporal process which takes place in six definite steps. But while no one would now dispute the process of evolution and the gradual formation of the world as we know it, few would argue that the first chapter of Genesis attempts to describe that process. In order to fill out and drive home his initial statement the author has to set the creation out in stages; however these stages are not chronological but rather dependent on a logical division (the three great areas of air, sea, land, and then their contents). The fact that the account is not really chronological at all brings out the fact that the Spirit is still today, so to speak, moving over formless chaos, that if the Spirit were not there everything would collapse into its hopeless lack of focus. Not only land, sea and air, but all the artefacts and products of man's genius would fall back into formlessness, which is another word for nothingness. More staggering yet, reason itself would fall apart, in a totally crazy, inconsequential jumble: the pride of man is his reason, and that at least he thinks to be his own, but this too is dependent on the Spirit of God. In one way it is a nightmare thought, for everything hangs, so to speak, by that one thread. But in another way the thought can fill one with confidence and trusting gratitude that the thread is so sure and firm, dependent not on our own unpredictable whims and moods but on the sureness of God's unmerited love.

In John's passage, the conversation with Nicodemus, comes the same combination of water and Spirit, but this time yielding not the world as such but rebirth. The implication is that this rebirth is to a totally new order of existence, as far removed from the first as that was from nothingness or formlessness. It gives an idea of the perfection to which we are called, of the dignity of this new creation. And yet there is no room for pride of self-congratulation, for the Spirit has absolute autonomy: it blows where it wills and those whom it recreates are subject to its direction, having nothing of themselves, but just picked up to be carried by the wind.

2

THE BREATH OF LIFE

Genesis 2:5-7

When no plant of the field was yet in the earth and no herb of the field had yet sprung up — for the Lord God had not caused it to rain upon the earth, and there was no man to till the ground; but a mist went up from the earth and watered the whole face of the ground — then the Lord God formed man of dust from the ground, and breathed into his nostrils the breath of life; and man became a living being.

John 19:25-30

Standing by the cross of Jesus were his mother, and his mother's sister, Mary the wife of Clopas, and Mary Magdalene. When Jesus saw his mother, and the disciple whom he loved standing near, he said to his mother, "Woman, behold, your son!" Then he said to the disciple, "Behold, your mother!" And from that hour the disciple took her to his own home.

After this Jesus, knowing that all was now finished, said (to fulfil the scripture), "I thirst". A bowl full of vinegar stood there; so they put a sponge full of the vinegar on hyssop and held it to his mouth. When Jesus had received the vinegar, he said, "It is finished"; and he bowed his head and gave up his spirit.

Reflection

The parallel between these two passages is quite striking: in the former the Creator breathes his own life into man; in the latter the Redeemer breathes forth his life upon the world.

It is only of man that this is said in the creation story. Of all the creatures it is said that he formed them (like a potter) from the clay, but for the others no further stage was required — that completed their formation. For man, however, the further step was needed which made him what he is, that God should breathe his own life into him. Man shares something of God, and so the special relationship is formed which means that man is destined for union with God and can find true happiness only in him. The anthropomorphic statement bypasses the philosopher's reasoning about the immortality of the soul, giving a pictorial image both less defined and emotionally richer, showing that that which makes man what he is gives him affinity of nature to God. Is this breath of man, received from God, the holy Spirit? We cannot, of course, say that man's life-principle is the third person of the Trinity, for man would then quite simply be divine. But in both Greek and Hebrew the same word means wind, breath and spirit, so in some sense God is breathing his own spirit into man.

The same ambiguity is used by John. In his long final discourse to his disciples Jesus had spoken so often of the Spirit which would come to his disciples to replace him, or rather to give them his presence among them, that the mention of 'his spirit' at the supreme moment of his parting from this earth must be significant. A more exact translation would be 'he handed over his spirit', and John, who so often thinks in double-meanings, surely means both that he handed over his spirit to his Father and that he gave it at that moment to his disciples. The moment of his passing from this world in death is the moment of his coming to the world in life: as he leaves it in the flesh, in all that is mortal, he comes to it in the spirit. The beauty of the image is that, like the image of the Creator breathing his life into man, it is open-ended: the breath is left, so to speak, hanging in the air, so that his spirit is breathed forth upon the whole world, for all to receive. He is no longer confined by time and space, the physical limits of a human being, but now is available and accessible through his spirit to all men, wherever and whenever they may be.

3

THE GLORY OF THE LORD

Ezekiel 10:18-19; 11:14-23

Then the glory of the Lord went forth from the
threshold of the house, and stood over the cherubim.
And the cherubim lifted up their wings and mounted
up from the earth in my sight as they went forth, with
the wheels beside them; and they stood at the door of
the east gate of the house of the Lord; and the glory
of the God of Israel was over them. . . .

And the word of the Lord came to me: "Son of
man, your brethren, even your brethren, your fellow
exiles, the whole house of Israel, all of them, are those
of whom the inhabitants of Jerusalem have said, 'They
have gone far from the Lord; to us this land is given
for a possession'. Therefore say, 'Thus says the Lord
God: Though I removed them far off among the
nations, and though I scattered them among the
countries, yet I have been a sanctuary to them for a
while in the countries where they have gone'. Therefore
say, 'Thus says the Lord God: I will gather you from
the peoples, and assemble you out of the countries where
you have been scattered, and I will give you the land
of Israel'. And when they come there, they will remove
from it all its detestable things and all its abominations.
And I will give them one heart, and put a new spirit
within them; I will take the stony heart out of their flesh,

B

and give them a heart of flesh, that they may walk in my statutes and keep my ordinances and obey them; and they shall be my people, and I will be their God. But as for those whose heart goes after their detestable things and their abominations, I will requite their deeds upon their own heads, says the Lord God."

Then the cherubim lifted up their wings, with the wheels beside them; and the glory of the God of Israel was over them. And the glory of the Lord went up from the midst of the city, and stood upon the mountain which is on the east side of the city.

1 Corinthians 6:15-20

Do you not know that your bodies are members of Christ? Shall I therefore take the members of Christ and make them members of a prostitute? Never! Do you not know that he who joins himself to a prostitute becomes one body with her? For, as it is written, "The two shall become one". But he who is united to the Lord becomes one spirit with him. Shun immorality. Every other sin which a man commits is outside the body; but the immoral man sins against his own body. Do you not know that your body is a temple of the Holy Spirit within you, which you have from God? You are not your own; you were bought with a price. So glorify God in your body.

Reflection

In the Old Testament Ezekiel sees in a vision the glory of the Lord leaving the temple; it is a sign of the end of the presence of God among men in the temple of Jerusalem and of the failure of the old covenant through

Israel's infidelities. In the middle, however, of the description of the visible departure of the glory of the Lord, Ezekiel puts the promise of a new and different presence of God among men: God will put a new spirit in them, when they have been purged and cleansed.

Paul draws the consequence of this: the presence of the new spirit makes us the temples of God, just as the old temple of Jerusalem was sanctified by the presence of God's glory and became pointless and vain when that presence had departed. Nor is it simply that the spirit of God dwells in us as a precious object lies in a case; we are possessed by the spirit. Paul cannot really distinguish between body and soul as a Greek philosopher can, considering the body as a sort of envelope for the soul. Man is not a soul in a body but is a live body, and the spirit is in that body not as in an envelope but as an element, surely *the* life-giving element. The horror for Paul of a Christian joining himself to a prostitute is that the act of intercourse is an act involving not merely the body but the whole person, including the element which is the holy spirit. Thus the whole temple is defiled. Worse, such an action is a jarring contradiction, for if the spirit is the life-giving principle, the life which it gives is a life consonant with its own nature. So also with the life of God; and in such an action it is being drawn into behaviour clean contrary to this.

The idea is further filled out in the last sentences of this passage from Corinthians. The Christian does not belong to himself but has been bought by Christ. This might seem an unjustified tyranny, except of course that we have offered ourselves to Christ and put ourselves in his power. It is through being the temples of the Spirit that we can glorify God, by doing his work in the world, acting not of ourselves but as his agents. The frightening responsibility of this appears when one

19

compares this to the Old Testament situation: in the Old Testament the glory of the Lord was to be found in his temple; in the new covenant his glory is to be found in his temples, Christians, and should shine forth through them. The Spirit of God must be as recognizable in Christians as it was in the temple of Jerusalem — or rather, more so, for it is a dynamic presence.

4

THE SPIRIT SEIZES UPON SAMSON

Judges 14:5-6

Then Samson went down with his father and mother
to Timnah, and he came to the vineyards of Timnah.
And behold, a young lion roared against him; and the
Spirit of the Lord came mightily upon him, and he tore
the lion asunder as one tears a kid; and he had nothing
in his hand. But he did not tell his father or his mother
what he had done.

1 Samuel 10:1-2, 5-13

Then Samuel took a vial of oil and poured it on his
head, and kissed him and said, "Has not the Lord
anointed you to be prince over his people Israel? And
you shall reign over the people of the Lord and you will
save them from the hand of their enemies round about.
And this shall be the sign to you that the Lord has
anointed you to be prince over his heritage. When you
depart from me today you will meet two men by Rachel's
tomb in the territory of Benjamin at Zelzah, and they
will say to you, 'The asses which you went to seek are
found, and now your father has ceased to care about
the asses and is anxious about you, saying, "What shall
I do about my son?"' . . . .

After that you shall come to Gibeathelohim, where there is a garrison of the Philistines; and there, as you come to the city, you will meet a band of prophets coming down from the high place with harp, tambourine, flute, and lyre before them, prophesying. Then the spirit of the Lord will come mightily upon you, and you shall prophesy with them and be turned into another man. Now when these signs meet you, do whatever your hand finds to do, for God is with you. And you shall go down before me to Gilgal; and behold, I am coming to you to offer burnt offerings and to sacrifice peace offerings. Seven days you shall wait, until I come to you and show you what you shall do."

When he turned his back to leave Samuel, God gave him another heart; and all these signs came to pass that day. When they came to Gibeah, behold, a band of prophets met him; and the spirit of God came mightily upon him, and he prophesied among them. And when all who knew him before saw how he prophesied with the prophets, the people said to one another, "What has come over the son of Kish? Is Saul also among the prophets?" And a man of the place answered, "And who is their father?" Therefore it became a proverb, "Is Saul also among the prophets?" When he had finished prophesying, he came to the high place.

Romans 15:17-19a

In Christ Jesus, then, I have reason to be proud of my work for God. For I will not venture to speak of anything except what Christ has wrought through me to win obedience from the Gentiles, by word and deed, by the power of signs and wonders, by the power of the Holy Spirit.

Reflection

The holy Spirit is a powerful force. In the Old Testament, when such phenomena were perhaps more necessary than they are now, it showed itself as a power which seized upon a man. It seized upon Samson and gave him superhuman strength, making him act like one demented. Just so it had seized on the other 'judges' in Israel, giving them a terrible power which enabled them to inspire and rally the flagging people and lead them to victory. When Saul is anointed with the Spirit it seizes on him too and leads him to join in with a band of ecstatic, dervish-like prophets. The Spirit is violent and can grip someone to take him right out of himself. In such cases it is almost more like a poltergeist than the gentle, benign Spirit of God, spreading peace to men, for it induced the leaders to violent, fierce action, demonstrations of the power of God. It was this Spirit, too, which inspired the companies of prophets which we meet in the Books of Kings, centred on Elijah and Elisha, living a strange life, separated from other men and bound together by the Spirit. For Paul also the Spirit is a fierce, compelling force which drives him on in his mission and enables him to work signs and wonders. The Spirit is not tamed and domesticated, calm and predictable, but is wild, frightening and awe-inspiring.

In our day too there is this element of overpowering someone in the speaking with tongues and other phenomena of the pentecostal movement. We cannot control the Spirit and have it do what we will and as we will, but must submit in the knowledge that, if we do, we are handing over control to one who is stronger than ourselves. It is not surprising, since the Spirit is God acting in the world, and God is an uncontrollable force. It is by means of these occasional, extraordinary demonstrations of the power of the Spirit that he shows the power of the Spirit which is always at work. The unpredictability of it, and the irresistible, almost savage, force makes one reflect what one is asking for by the innocuous and oft-repeated request to the holy Spirit to come and fill our hearts: it is an invitation to an uncontrollable torrent to break its dam and overwhelm us.

5

THE SPIRIT WHO PROCEEDS
FROM THE FATHER

Wisdom 7:22—8:1

For wisdom is in herself a spirit that is intelligent, holy,
unique, manifold, subtle,
mobile, clear, unpolluted,
distinct, invulnearable, loving the good, keen,
irresistible, beneficent, human,
steadfast, sure, free from anxiety,
all-powerful, overseeing all,
and penetrating through all spirits
that are intelligent and pure and most subtle.
For wisdom is more mobile than any motion;
because of her pureness she pervades and penetrates
    all things.
For she is a breath of the power of God,
and a pure emanation of the glory of the Almighty;
therefore nothing defiled gains entrance into her.
For she is a reflection of eternal light,
a spotless mirror of the working of God,
and an image of his goodness.
Though she is but one, she can do all things,
and while remaining in herself, she renews all things;
in every generation she passes into holy souls
and makes them friends of God, and prophets;

for God loves nothing so much as the man who lives
    with wisdom.
For she is more beautiful than the sun,
and excels every constellation of the stars.
Compared with the light she is found to be superior,
for it is succeeded by the night,
but against wisdom evil does not prevail.
She reaches mightily from one end of the earth
    to the other,
and she orders all things well.

John 15:26-27

But when the Counsellor comes, whom I shall send to
you from the Father, even the Spirit of truth, who
proceeds from the Father, he will bear witness to me;
and you also are witnesses, because you have been with
me from the beginning.

Reflection

The passage from the Book of Wisdom describes the
wisdom of God. In the preparation at the end of the
Old Testament for the revelation of the Trinity, God
was regarded as acting in the world by his wisdom. This
idea of God's wisdom was really arrived at through
meditation on the wisdom which man receives from
God, and which can then be seen to be the spirit of
God working in man and guiding him. The highest and
latest stage of Old Testament revelation about the
spirit is the passage in Wisdom: wisdom, a spirit from
God, has all the qualities of God himself, all-powerful
and all-pervading, beneficent and loving the good. It is
impossible to say whether wisdom is separate from God
or an aspect of God, for it is as though the images used

want to express both and exclude neither. Hence wisdom is 'a breath of the power of God' and so would seem to be intimately one with God, and yet she is also an 'emanation of the glory of the Almighty', so should perhaps be said to issue forth into a separate existence. As an 'image of his goodness' wisdom might seem to be identical but distinguishable, but as 'a reflection of eternal light' to be inseparable from the light itself. The ambiguity here comes very close to expressing and filling out what we mean when we say that the Spirit has one nature with the Father but is a different person.

And yet is it the Spirit that is meant here? Paul refers some of the key expressions to Christ: he is the image of the Father's goodness and the reflection of the eternal light, and it seems that Paul regards Christ as the wisdom of the Father. The solution is that it is not strictly correct to assign the work of God in the world to any one of the persons of the Trinity specifically — apart from the incarnate Christ — and apart from this it is not easy to make the distinction between the second and third persons of the Trinity. Both are originated rather than originator, and in closest union with the originator, as this passage from the Book of Wisdom shows.

Christ says the same in the passage from John: just as he does, the Spirit proceeds from the Father. The Spirit bears witness to Christ and continues among his disciples the same work which he himself did on earth. The Spirit is, so to speak, a second Christ who is with us still.

6

THE TRINITY

Psalm 20(19):1-5

The Lord answer you in the day of trouble!
The name of the God of Jacob protect you!
May he send you help from the sanctuary,
    and give you support from Zion!
May he remember all your offerings,
    and regard with favour your burnt sacrifices!
May he grant you your heart's desire,
    and fulfil all your plans!
May we shout for joy over your victory,
    and in the name of our God set up our banners!
May the Lord fulfil all your petitions!

2 Corinthians 13:14

The grace of the Lord Jesus Christ and the love of God
and the fellowship of the Holy Spirit be with you all.

Reflection

One might begin to wonder whether the Spirit is really
God; there seem to be so many situations in which the
Spirit seems to be merely the tool of God. The Spirit

is, perhaps, a person, as Christ is a person; but is it divine? The New Testament is very chary about calling even Christ God, and does it unequivocally only three times (each of these being in a late passage, the product of much reflection). About the Spirit it seems to be even more inexplicit.

Yet dotted about the New Testament are such passages as these, where all three persons are put on a level. By the triple formula some equality is implied. In the blessing with which the second letter to the Corinthians concludes, Paul prays that the love of all three persons may come down, in a different way for each. The 'grace' of the Lord Jesus Christ translates the Greek *charis*, which contains the idea of liberality and undeservedness; it is the word used of a gift lavished by a sovereign on a subject without any merits or deserts on the part of the subject: so the love is to be a totally free gift bestowed entirely from the open-handed good pleasure of the Lord Christ. The word used for the 'love' of God is warm and devoted; it implies a self-giving even at expense and hardship to oneself, very often in response to a family relationship: it is the real thoughtful care of the Father for his beloved children. The 'fellowship' of the holy Spirit is the most intimate, for it is an actual participation in the holy Spirit. But the meaning does not stop there; it is left open: the sharing is in the holy Spirit, having a share in him, but also having through this participation a share in God and in each other. It is as though the Spirit *is* the love which binds all together. For the expressions 'sharing' and 'participation' are too reserved and niggardly; what is meant is really unitedness or oneness. Paul is surely aware that he leaves the exact object open: the holy Spirit is the bond of Christians, the bond to God in his giving, and the bond to the fellow-Christians who share the same bond to make their oneness.

7

SEALED WITH THE SPIRIT

Ephesians 1:3-14

Blessed be the God and Father of our Lord Jesus Christ, who has blessed us in Christ with every spiritual blessing in the heavenly places, even as he chose us in him before the foundation of the world, that we should be holy and blameless before him. He destined us in love to be his sons through Jesus Christ, according to the purpose of his will, to the praise of his glorious grace which he freely bestowed on us in the Beloved. In him we have redemption through his blood, the forgiveness of our trespasses, according to the riches of his grace which he lavished upon us. For he has made known to us in all wisdom and insight the mystery of his will, according to his purpose which he set forth in Christ as a plan for the fullness of time, to unite all things in him, things in heaven and things on earth.

In him, according to the purpose of him who accomplishes all things according to the counsel of his will, we who first hoped in Christ have been destined and appointed to live for the praise of his glory. In him you also, who have heard the word of truth, the gospel of your salvation, and have believed in him, were sealed with the promised Holy Spirit, who is the guarantee of our inheritance until we acquire possession of it, to the praise of his glory.

Reflection

Paul begins the letter to the Ephesians with this ample hymn, in which he describes the part of each of the persons of the Trinity in our salvation. God the Father is the initiator: he chose us and predestined us in love to be his sons, and revealed to us the mystery of his will. All this, however, is in Christ Jesus: it is in him that we are chosen and are sons of God, and in him that the mystery is revealed, since it was God's will to unite all things in him. A fuller translation of this phrase would bring out that Christ is the head of all things and the principle of them all, which makes sense out of them all: without him creation cannot achieve its end or make full sense.

Slipped in, seemingly, at the end is the third person, the Spirit. But in fact, so far as we are concerned, he is the climax of the hymn: the sealing with the Spirit is the guarantee of all that precedes. In the ancient world marking with a seal was used as a sign of ownership, so that being sealed with the Spirit of God means belonging finally to God. Furthermore a seal with a divine representation on it dedicated the thing sealed to the divinity and placed it under the deity's special protection, warding off all interference. So if we are sealed with the Spirit by that means we belong irrevocably to God and are marked out for his protection. In the ancient Church baptism is often referred to as this seal.

At the end the Spirit is also called 'the guarantee of our inheritance'. The word is drawn from ancient commercial language and really means a first instalment which is a guarantee of those which are to follow. In sealing us as belonging to God, the Spirit also gives us the first instalment of our heritage. This is how the writer solves that Pauline puzzle whether we are risen and transformed already — as in one sense we are, as soon as we belong to the risen Christ — or whether the transformation is still to come: we are not wholly formed into new creatures yet, but the work has begun by the pledge of the Spirit in such a way as to guarantee the completion of the work. We are, by this sealing, under the regime of the Spirit, and in his hands to make us wholly God's.

8

SONS OF GOD BY THE SPIRIT

Exodus 4:21-23

And the Lord said to Moses, "When you go back to Egypt, see that you do before Pharaoh all the miracles which I have put in your power; but I will harden his heart, so that he will not let the people go. And you shall say to Pharaoh, 'Thus says the Lord, Israel is my first-born son, and I say to you, "Let my son go that he may serve me"; if you refuse to let him go, behold, I will slay your first-born son.' "

Hosea 11:1-4

When Israel was a child, I loved him,
 and out of Egypt I called my son.
The more I called them,
 the more they went from me;
they kept sacrificing to the Baals,
 and burning incense to idols.
Yet it was I who taught Ephraim to walk,
 I took them up in my arms;
 but they did not know that I healed them.
I led them with cords of compassion,
 with the bands of love,

and I became to them as one
  who eases the yoke on their jaws,
  and I bent down to them and fed them.

Romans 8:14-17

For all who are led by the Spirit of God are sons of God.
For you did not receive the spirit of slavery to fall back
into fear, but you have received the spirit of sonship.
When we cry, "Abba! Father!" it is the Spirit himself
bearing witness with our spirit that we are children of
God, and if children, then heirs, heirs of God and
fellow heirs with Christ, provided we suffer with him
in order that we may also be glorified with him.

Reflection

To be sons of God is staggering, though as with so many
truths of Christian theology, familiarity has blinded us
to the degree of this privilege. It was already striking
enough in the Old Testament, when God took Israel to
himself in a unique way, differentiating it from all other
nations and calling it — in the exodus story — his son.
The people of Israel were well aware that their link
with Yahweh was closer than that of any other nation
with their protecting god; the fullness of this relationship comes to be seen in the Book of Hosea, when the
prophet lingers over the fatherly care which Yahweh
lavishes on his son Israel.

Since there can be no question of physical paternity
with God, it must always be determined what exactly
is meant by calling someone 'son of God'. The Bible
denotes thereby various states, but each one is a very
special personal relationship with God. There is Israel,

the people God chose to be his own, or the king who is the spearhead of the people in their relationship to God and God's special representative to the people, so under his special care and guidance. Above all there is the Messiah who is God's son in a unique sense because he is to be God's unique representative in the completion of God's final plan, coming to do the work which is often described as the work of God himself. And in the event the relationship was more special yet, for the Messiah had the powers and personality of God himself, and so could truly be said to be within the divinity itself. His unique relationship to the Father comes out most clearly in the prayers of loving surrender and union which John preserves for us, and also in the prayer in the garden when he addresses his Father by the intimate name 'Abba', the word of affection used by young children to their father.

It is this closeness of relationship which the Spirit gives us. By having the Spirit within us we are brought into the family of God. Our relationship with him is one of family intimacy, the trust and loving dependence of the young child on its father, knowing that the ties of blood — or in our case of the Spirit — constitute a sure claim on his love and care.

9

JESUS AND THE SPIRIT

Isaiah 42:1-4

Behold my servant, whom I uphold,
  my chosen, in whom my soul delights;
I have put my Spirit upon him,
  he will bring forth justice to the nations.
He will not cry or lift up his voice,
  or make it heard in the street;
a bruised reed he will not break,
  and a dimly burning wick he will not quench;
  he will faithfully bring forth justice.
He will not fail or be discouraged
  till he has established justice in the earth;
  and the coastlands wait for his law.

Mark 1:9-11

In those days Jesus came from Nazareth of Galilee and
was baptized by John in the Jordan. And when he came
up out of the water, immediately he saw the heavens
opened and the Spirit descending upon him like a dove;
and a voice came from heaven, "Thou art my beloved
Son; with thee I am well pleased."

Reflection

The first Song of the Servant of the Lord in Isaiah describes a mysterious figure who is to carry out the Lord's mission of bringing justice to the earth, that is, restoring the world to the state which God willed for it, undoing the disorders of sin. He is to do this with the gentleness of God himself, coaxing rather than obliterating the dimly burning flame, making the most of what there is.

For this purpose the Servant is given the Spirit of the Lord. As one sees from the occasions when the Spirit seized on Gideon or Samson or Saul, the Spirit is given always for a purpose, in connection with a mission. It is not a passive gift to the recipient but is an empowering, enabling him to do the work of God. The Spirit seized upon Gideon and Saul to guide them to drive back the enemies of God's people; it rests upon the Servant to enable him to accomplish God's mission of healing and restoration. Both are the work of the Spirit, but perhaps one might say that, since our natural aggressiveness and selfishness incline us more to the former kind of action, one needs the help of the Spirit more obviously and more frequently for the work of healing and restoring.

The baptism of Christ is the moment when he received the Spirit of God for his messianic mission. Until then his life had been one of preparation, submission to the will of his Father in obscurity and reflection upon the work he was called upon to do. In Mark's gospel it is clear that the descent of the Spirit is a sign to him, not to the multitudes. The final words of the voice could equally well be translated 'in you my soul delights', so that the whole scene would immediately recall the passage of Isaiah. It showed Jesus, then, what was the Spirit he was receiving, and what was the mission as Messiah. It was not, as some thought, to exterminate the wicked and glorify the pious, nor to introduce an era of everlasting feasting and merriment. It was the humble and gentle mission of a Servant, fulfilling the unglamorous and often heart-breaking task of trying to mend what is broken and save what is nearly lost, thus serving God and men.

It was in this mission as a servant that he called all Christians to follow him — giving his life to save many — and it was this Spirit which he gave to Christians, to use if we will.

10

THE BIRTH OF THE CHURCH

Exodus 19:17-19; 20:18-21

Then Moses brought the people out of the camp to meet God; and they took their stand at the foot of the mountain. And Mount Sinai was wrapped in smoke, because the Lord descended upon it in fire; and the smoke of it went up like the smoke of a kiln, and the whole mountain quaked greatly. And as the sound of the trumpet grew louder and louder, Moses spoke, and God answered him in thunder. . . .

Now when all the people perceived the thunderings and the lightnings and the sound of the trumpet and the mountain smoking, the people were afraid and trembled; and they stood afar off, and said to Moses, "You speak to us, and we will hear; but let not God speak to us, lest we die." And Moses said to the people, "Do not fear; for God has come to prove you, and that the fear of him may be before your eyes, that you may not sin."

And the people stood afar off, while Moses drew near to the thick darkness where God was.

Acts 2:1-12

When the day of Pentecost had come, they were all together in one place. And suddenly a sound came from heaven like the rush of a mighty wind, and it filled all the house where they were sitting. And there appeared to them tongues as of fire, distributed and resting on each one of them. And they were all filled with the Holy Spirit and began to speak in other tongues, as the Spirit gave them utterance.

Now there were dwelling in Jerusalem Jews, devout men from every nation under heaven. And at this sound the multitude came together, and they were bewildered, because each one heard them speaking in his own language. And they were amazed and wondered, saying, "Are not all these who are speaking Galileans? And how is it that we hear, each of us in his own native language? Parthians and Medes and Elamites and residents of Mesopotamia, Judea and Cappadocia, Pontus and Asia, Phrygia and Pamphylia, Egypt and the parts of Libya belonging to Cyrene, and visitors from Rome, both Jews and proselytes, Cretans and Arabians, we hear them telling in our own tongues the mighty works of God." And all were amazed and perplexed, saying to one another, "What does this mean?"

Reflection

The scene on Sinai is in a very real sense the birth of Israel as a nation, because there Moses makes the covenant with God when he has revealed himself in this awesome fashion, and it is the covenant with God which makes Israel what it is. The central fact of the covenant is that God binds himself to be with Israel, to stand by them and remain in their midst, as he does by his presence in the Tent of Meeting.

In his account of the coming of the Spirit at Pentecost Luke uses some of the imagery of the Sinai event, especially that the Lord descended on the mountain in fire. Similarly the 'sound from heaven' recalls the description of the scene in Deuteronomy (4:36). The peoples drawn from all over the known world provide another point of contact, for it was a rabbinic tradition that the voice of God, heard on that day, divided itself into tongues to be understood by all the nations of the world. So Luke is showing that this event is the birth of the Church, just as the descent of God on Mount Sinai was the birth of Israel. And in each case it is the presence of God which is the permanent effect that gives life to the nation thus called into being; in the New Testament instance this presence is the presence of the Spirit. Throughout the account of the earliest history of the Church which is the Acts of the Apostles we are constantly reminded of the presence, active and guiding, of the Spirit. He guides the community life of the early community in Jerusalem; he sends Paul off on his missionary journeys, and guides him explicitly at each important turning-point; he inspires the deliberations of the leaders of the Church when important decisions are to be made, and so on.

What makes the Church what it is, then, is the Spirit. The pomp and magnificence or the lowliness and weakness of its material institutions, even the nobility or faultiness of its ministers and members, are only a distracting shell. What matters is the Spirit of God whose descent brought the Church to life, and the only criterion in the Church is how far this Spirit is allowed its freedom and expression in its members.

11

DRUNK WITH THE SPIRIT

Joel 2:27-32

You shall know that I am in the midst of Israel,
    and that I, the Lord, am your God
        and there is none else.
And my people shall never again be put to shame.

And it shall come to pass afterward,
    that I will pour out my spirit on all flesh;
your sons and your daughters shall prophesy,
    your old men shall dream dreams,
    and your young men shall see visions.
Even upon the menservants and maidservants
    in those days, I will pour out my spirit.

And I will give portents in the heavens and on
the earth, blood and fire and columns of smoke. The
sun shall be turned to darkness, and the moon to blood,
before the great and terrible day of the Lord comes.
And it shall come to pass that all who call upon the
name of the Lord shall be delivered; for in Mount Zion
and in Jerusalem there shall be those who escape, as
the Lord has said, and among the survivors shall be
those whom the Lord calls.

But Peter, standing with the eleven, lifted up his voice and addressed them, "Men of Judea and all who dwell in Jerusalem, let this be known to you, and give ear to my words. For these men are not drunk, as you suppose, since it is only the third hour of the day; but this is what was spoken by the prophet Joel:

'And in the last days it shall be, God declares,
that I will pour out my Spirit upon all flesh,
and your sons and your daughters shall prophesy,
and your young men shall see visions,
and your old men shall dream dreams;
yea, and on my menservants and my maidservants
    in those days
I will pour out my Spirit; and they shall prophesy.
And I will show wonders in the heaven above
and signs on the earth beneath,
blood, and fire, and vapour of smoke;
the sun shall be turned into darkness
and the moon into blood,
before the day of the Lord comes,
the great and manifest day.
And it shall be that whoever calls on the name of
    the Lord shall be saved' . . . .

Now when they heard this they were cut to the heart, and said to Peter and the rest of the apostles, "Brethren, what shall we do?" And Peter said to them, "Repent, and be baptized every one of you in the name of Jesus Christ for the forgiveness of your sins; and you shall receive the gift of the Holy Spirit."

Reflection

The prophet Joel is describing the extraordinary events which were expected when God came to dwell among his people in the renewal of all things at the end of the world. The general import is that the most certain things in nature, the light of the sun and the paleness of the moon, will be turned upside down, and there will be a terrifying reversal of nature. At the same time those faithful to the Lord, who turn to him for deliverance, will be given extraordinary powers associated with being possessed by God as the ecstatic prophets were.

How far was this fulfilled by the actual events? The coming of the Spirit at Pentecost is clearly marked in the Acts as this definitive coming of God among his people, and the author regards the event as the birth of the Church and so the beginning of the final era of the world, the winding-up period after the decisive event, when there are just loose ends to be tidied. Part of the meaning of Joel was that the coming of God was to be a judgment, a great divide when all but those who call upon the name of the Lord are doomed to destruction in the general cataclysm of nature, while these latter are by contrast endowed with divine powers. In just this way John's gospel especially looks upon the coming of Christ as the great divide, when the majority condemn themselves by rejecting him, while those who accept him win divine life. In Acts, however, it is the moment of the coming of the Spirit which is the moment of judgment, when the apostles are filled with the powers of which Joel had spoken, and the masses of people hasten to be saved by calling upon the name of the Lord.

Another item in the story of the coming of the Spirit deserves consideration: the apostles are accused of being drunk. This is partly the result of their speaking in tongues. But it also underlines the unpredictability of the Spirit. There is no submitting oneself to the rule of the Spirit on limited terms; he may lead in ways which seem contrary to all good sense and sober conduct, where only a madman would follow. Sometimes we can recognize this as abandonment to the folly of the Cross, and only pray to have the courage to follow. Sometimes the prophet and the charlatan are indistinguishable, and this fact gives us an excuse for refusing to be guided by the Spirit and expose ourselves too to the accusation of being drunk.

12

WHAT MAKES A CHRISTIAN?

Acts 11:1-4, 11-18

Now the apostles and the brethren who were in Judea heard that the Gentiles also had received the word of God. So when Peter went up to Jerusalem, the circumcision party criticized him, saying, "Why did you go to uncircumcised men and eat with them?" But Peter began and explained to them in order. . . .

"At that very moment three men arrived at the house in which we were, sent to me from Caesarea. And the Spirit told me to go with them, making no distinction. These six brethren also accompanied me, and we entered the man's house. And he told us how he had seen the angel standing in his house and saying, 'Send to Joppa and bring Simon called Peter; he will declare to you a message by which you will be saved, you and all your household.' As I began to speak, the Holy Spirit fell on them just as on us at the beginning. And I remembered the word of the Lord, how he said, 'John baptized with water, but you shall be baptized with the Holy Spirit.' If then God gave the same gift to them as he gave to us when we believed in the Lord Jesus Christ, who was I that could withstand God?" When they heard this they were silenced. And they glorified God, saying, "Then to the Gentiles also God has granted repentance unto life."

Acts 19:1-6

While Apollos was at Corinth, Paul passed through the upper country and came to Ephesus. There he found some disciples. And he said to them, "Did you receive the Holy Spirit when you believed?" And they said, "No, we have never even heard that there is a Holy Spirit." And he said, "Into what then were you baptized?" They said, "Into John's baptism." And Paul said, "John baptized with the baptism of repentance, telling the people to believe in the one who was to come after him, that is, Jesus." On hearing this, they were baptized in the name of the Lord Jesus. And when Paul had laid his hands upon them, the Holy Spirit came on them; and they spoke with tongues and prophesied.

Galatians 3:1-5

O foolish Galatians! Who has bewitched you, before whose eyes Jesus Christ was publicly portrayed as crucified? Let me ask you only this: Did you receive the Spirit by works of the law, or by hearing with faith? Are you so foolish? Having begun with the Spirit, are you now ending with the flesh? Did you experience so many things in vain? — if it really is in vain. Does he who supplies the Spirit to you and works miracles among you do so by works of the law, or by hearing with faith?

Reflection

In all these passages the message is the same: what makes a Christian is the coming to him of the holy Spirit. In the first passage Peter's point is that Cornelius, though a gentile, cannot be excluded from the Christian community because the Spirit has come upon him even without Peter's or anyone else's agency; the baptism of the centurion and his household is no more than a formality, a sort of official confirmation. The disciples of John at Ephesus obviously have something wrong with their Christianity, and this is immediately and strikingly rectified when they receive the Spirit. In Galatians Paul assumes as a basic fact that Christians have the Spirit; it is not only a fact but an empirical one, for he can appeal to the phenomena which go with it, and which all can witness.

Thus the basic fact about a Christian is not that he has been baptized or received the sacraments; it is not that he puts his salvation in Christ, though this no doubt is a necessary condition; it is simply that he has been possessed by the Spirit. Just as in the community of the Church the central factor is that the Church draws its life from the presence of the Spirit, so for the individual his life-principle is the Spirit. In speaking of the resurrection Paul contrasts those whose life-principle is the soul (the life-principle of man as such) and those whose life-principle is the Spirit. Their life is transformed and already transferred to the sphere of the divine: it already has the glory of the divine, its permanence and its power. Such is the life of the Christian because he already, even in this life, has the Spirit as his life-principle.

This is all very well in our better moments, and especially in moments of reflection when we are at peace with ourselves and free from the annoyances of contact with others. But even then we can remember that the Spirit does not always get his way with us, that though he is our life-principle, he is yet too often cramped by conflicting interests, selfishnesses and passion.

13

THE SPIRIT OF TRUTH

Jeremiah 31:31-34

"Behold, the days are coming, says the Lord, when I will make a new covenant with the house of Israel and the house of Judah, not like the covenant which I made with their fathers when I took them by the hand to bring them out of the land of Egypt, my covenant which they broke, though I was their husband, says the Lord. But this is the covenant which I will make with the house of Israel after those days, says the Lord: I will put my law within them, and I will write it upon their hearts; and I will be their God, and they shall be my people. And no longer shall each man teach his neighbour and each his brother, saying, 'Know the Lord', for they shall all know me, from the least of them to the greatest, says the Lord; for I will forgive their iniquity, and I will remember their sin no more."

John 16:7, 12-15

Nevertheless I tell you the truth: it is to your advantage that I go away, for if I do not go away, the Counsellor will not come to you; but if I go, I will send him to you. . . .

I have yet many things to say to you, but you cannot bear them now. When the Spirit of truth comes, he will guide you into all the truth; for he will not speak on his own authority, but whatever he hears he will speak, and he will declare to you the things that are to come. He will glorify me, for he will take what is mine and declare it to you. All that the Father has is mine; therefore I said that he will take what is mine and declare it to you.

Reflection

Jeremiah promised that in the renewal of the covenant it would not be as in the old covenant when the individual derived all from the institutions of the nation, but each individual would have the Law engraved on his heart. The Spirit is with each one of us, leading us all into the complete truth. This gives rise to two reflections.

Even the apostles to whom Jesus was speaking at the last supper were not capable of bearing the full truth. It was only after the resurrection and ascension that they began to realize the full import of Jesus' words, and through the first Christian generation one can see the Church penetrating more deeply into Christ's message. Only gradually did they come to realize the full truth about Christ's divinity, and even to the end of the New Testament era were hesitant to call Jesus 'God'. At first they seem to have expected the second coming of Christ in the immediate future and only when this failed to occur did they realize that they were looking in the wrong direction and that Christ had been with them all the time. This is how the Spirit led them gradually into the full truth. And yet one can never say that we have reached the full truth, for constantly the Church grows out of limitations in her view of the message of Christ and penetrates more deeply into its meaning — just as individuals do also in their understanding and appreciation. This it is which makes our faith a living faith and the Church a living organism, constantly growing and, in virtue of its own life-principle, able to draw nourishment and assimilate into its own richness the surrounding world in which it grows. The difference between this and a dead, petrified religion is the Spirit which leads into all truth, continuing the revelation from the Father, and so his glorification.

A second reflection is on the relationship between the individual and the whole in the new covenant. One might think that if each of God's people has the Law inscribed on their hearts there is no need for a teaching Church. Indeed the voice of the Church is composed of the united voice of all her individual members, who all testify to the same truth. But as in any human situation the members of an organic whole have different parts to play, so in the Church; and the Spirit guides each according to his position in the Church. Can one say that the Pope is more guided by the Spirit than any random believer? No, each is guided according to his function in the Church, the random believer no less than the teacher, but in a different way.

14

FREEDOM IN THE SPIRIT

Galatians 5:13-26

For you were called to freedom, brethren; only do not
use your freedom as an opportunity for the flesh, but
through love be servants of one another. For the whole
law is fulfilled in one word, "You shall love your neighbour as yourself." But if you bite and devour one
another take heed that you are not consumed by one
another.

But I say, walk by the Spirit, and do not gratify the
desires of the flesh. For the desires of the flesh are
against the Spirit, and the desires of the Spirit are
against the flesh; for these are opposed to each other,
to prevent you from doing what you would. But if you
are led by the Spirit you are not under the law. Now
the works of the flesh are plain: immorality, impurity,
licentiousness, idolatry, sorcery, enmity, strife, jealousy,
anger, selfishness, dissension, party spirit, envy, drunken-
ness, carousing, and the like. I warn you, as I warned
you before, that those who do such things shall not
inherit the kingdom of God. But the fruit of the Spirit
is love, joy, peace, patience, kindness, goodness, faith-
fulness, gentleness, self-control; against such there is
no law. And those who belong to Christ Jesus have
crucified the flesh with its passions and desires.

If we live by the Spirit, let us also walk by the Spirit. Let us have no self-conceit, no provoking of one another, no envy of one another.

1 Corinthians 6:12-14

"All things are lawful for me," but not all things are helpful. "All things are lawful for me," but I will not be enslaved by anything. "Food is meant for the stomach and the stomach for food" — and God will destroy both one and the other. The body is not meant for immorality, but for the Lord, and the Lord for the body. And God raised the Lord and will also raise us up by his power.

1 Corinthians 10:23-24

"All things are lawful," but not all things are helpful. "All things are lawful," but not all things build up. Let no one seek his own good, but the good of his neighbour. Eat whatever is sold in the meat market without raising any question on the ground of conscience.

Reflection

All through the letter to the Galatians Paul has been contrasting the regime of the Spirit with the regime of the Law, showing how the Law was a temporary situation and restrictive. Towards the end he compares life under the Law and under the Spirit to the status of slave and that of free man. The Corinthians, too, were obviously familiar with this distinction, for they proclaimed that they were free of all rules and regulations, using as their slogan 'all things are lawful'. The same sort of spirit is alive in the contemporary scorn for laws and rules in religious matters; it is stressed that such things are for children and adult Christians are above these petty rulings.

Paul, however, is a realist. He recognizes, and rejoices in, the fact that the Christian's rule of life is the Spirit, an interior force rather than an exterior restriction, a motive power rather than a restraining harness. But he realizes that there is another power at work, the flesh, by which he means all the unredeemed tendencies in man which are not subject to God. The flesh is not primarily a sensual and sexual force but reaches to what we would consider primarily mental and spiritual tendencies — though it is hard to make an absolute distinction.

When he speaks of being led by the Spirit, and of the fruits of the Spirit, with a list of actions and attitudes, what he envisages is that there is no compulsion necessary because if one is subject to the Spirit this willing subjection necessarily issues spontaneously in one kind of action. Such action is a sign that it is the Spirit and not the flesh which is the mainspring and the driving-force; against such there is no law because no coercion is necessary.

Again and again in Paul's lists of fruits of the Spirit, if one tries to find the basis, it always turns out to be attitudes towards one's neighbour. This is particularly clear in Galatians, but also in the second passage from Corinthians, where the Corinthians are told that they must restrict their legitimate liberty for the sake of the weak consciences of others. But also in the first passage from Corinthians in the last analysis sexual restraint is the natural outcome of personal relationships with Christ and with other people.

15

THE NEW LIFE OF THE SPIRIT

Ezekiel 37:1-14

The hand of the Lord was upon me, and he brought me out by the Spirit of the Lord, and set me down in the midst of the valley; it was full of bones. And he led me round among them; and behold, there were very many upon the valley; and lo, they were very dry. And he said to me, "Son of man, can these bones live?" And I answered, "O Lord God, thou knowest." Again he said to me, "Prophesy to these bones, and say to them, O dry bones, hear the word of the Lord. Thus says the Lord God to these bones: Behold, I will cause breath to enter you, and you shall live. And I will lay sinews upon you, and will cause flesh to come upon you, and cover you with skin, and put breath in you, and you shall live; and you shall know that I am the Lord."

So I prophesised as I was commanded; and as I prophesied, there was a noise, and behold, a rattling; and the bones came together, bone to its bone. And as I looked, there were sinews on them, and flesh had come upon them, and skin had covered them; but there was no breath in them. Then he said to me, "Prophesy to the breath, prophesy, son of man, and say to the breath, Thus says the Lord God: Come from the four winds, O breath, and breathe upon these slain, that they may live." So I prophesied as he commanded me, and the breath came into them, and they lived, and stood upon their feet, an exceedingly great host.

Then he said to me, "Son of man, these bones are the whole house of Israel. Behold, they say, 'Our bones are dried up, and our hope is lost; we are clean cut off.' Therefore prophesy, and say to them, Thus says the Lord God: Behold, I will open your graves, and raise you from your graves, O my people; and I will bring you home into the land of Israel. And you shall know that I am the Lord, when I open your graves, and raise you from your graves, O my people. And I will put my Spirit within you, and you shall live, and I will place you in your own land; then you shall know that I, the Lord, have spoken, and I have done it, says the Lord."

John 20:19-23

On the evening of that day, the first day of the week, the doors being shut where the disciples were, for fear of the Jews, Jesus came and stood among them and said to them, "Peace be with you." When he had said this, he showed them his hands and his side. Then the disciples were glad when they saw the Lord. Jesus said to them again, "Peace be with you. As the Father has sent me, even so I send you." And when he had said this, he breathed on them, and said to them, "Receive the Holy Spirit. If you forgive the sins of any, they are forgiven; if you retain the sins of any, they are retained."

Reflection

Ezekiel's vision is a promise of the restoration of Israel: Israel seemed to be dead in her captivity, represented by the bleached bones in the valley, but when the Spirit of God breathes upon these bones, they rise to a new life. The promise is fulfilled in the scene in John after the resurrection, when, Jesus breathes his Spirit upon the disciples. This is the moment at which they receive the new life which has been the theme of so much of Jesus' teaching during his ministry. He had spoken so constantly of the eternal life which he would give to those who believed in him. Eternal life is in his words, to be found in the bread of life which comes down from heaven; he *is* resurrection and life. Now at his resurrection he breathes on them and gives them this life by giving them his holy Spirit.

If this is a correct view, it seems strange that Christ should go straight on to the power to forgive sins. But the link is that the Jews always associated the forgiveness of sins with the outpouring of the Spirit which was to occur at the last time. Israel was to rise from the dead bones as a purified nation. Forgiveness is not simply a legal action, as though a slate was wiped clean: the sin that there was is replaced by the Spirit. Sin is not simply a black spot on the soul, but is an alienation from God; when the alienation is removed there replaces it, by the very fact of the removal of the alienation, a closer relationship to God. Conversely, the Spirit is not simply a lump of gold or valuable substance, or even a power; the Spirit *is* the presence of God, and where the Spirit is, there is a close relationship with God. Receiving the Spirit, being forgiven one's sins and entering into the friendship of God are different expressions for the same reality.

E

16

THE PARACLETE

John 14:15-21

If you love me, you will keep my commandments. And I will pray the Father, and he will give you another Counsellor, to be with you for ever, even the Spirit of truth, whom the world cannot receive, because it neither sees him nor knows him; you know him, for he dwells with you, and will be in you.

I will not leave you desolate; I will come to you. Yet a little while, and the world will see me no more, but you will see me; because I live, you will live also. In that day you will know that I am in my Father, and you in me, and I in you. He who has my commandments and keeps them, he it is who loves me; and he who loves me will be loved by my Father, and I will love him and manifest myself to him.

Reflection

Who is this Counsellor whom the Father will send? Only John uses the expression, and apart from one passage in his first epistle (where the expression obviously has a different reference, since it is used of Jesus now in heaven and pleading for us) even he uses it only in

Jesus' address after the last supper. The Greek word 'paraclete' means basically one called to be beside someone as a help and assistance; this is probably as far as it is useful to go in defining the word. For usually the word has the sense of an advocate in court, and though the Paraclete will inspire Christians in their defence of the truth, the Paraclete is usually thought of as an advocate in the judgment of heaven. Closer to the Christian use is the related word *paraclesis,* which is used of the encouragement and support given to Christians especially in times of trial and persecution; but this again is not the central function of the Paraclete in John. No better is the expression 'Counsellor' used in this RSV translation.

The Paraclete will continue to do the work of Jesus: he is *'another* Paraclete', suggesting that there had been a first; his coming will mean that the disciples are not left orphans; he will lead the disciples to the fullness of Jesus' message, instructing them in the truth which they are not yet ready to bear. In the same way as Jesus, the Paraclete will have a hostile reception from the world — the world cannot accept him nor recognize him — in contrast to the disciples in whom he dwells. In all these respects the Paraclete is like Jesus.

In some way also the coming of the Paraclete is the coming of Jesus. It is in connection with the coming of the Paraclete that Jesus says he is going away for a little while, only to return again to his disciples. And in the present passage he suggests that the disciples will see him because they live and he lives — and they live by the Spirit.

The Paraclete is the Spirit of truth. One cannot say that the Paraclete is Jesus, nor yet does it seem close enough to say that the Paraclete is the Spirit of Jesus. As the Paraclete is obviously a person one cannot say that it is the spirit of Jesus (without a capital, as one speaks of the spirit of adventure, or the spirit of an assembly). Perhaps it is best to leave it vague — after all, one gospel says that John the Baptist was Elijah, and another denies it, so that he was and he wasn't — for the central fact is that the Paraclete makes Jesus present to us by carrying on his work in us now.

17

THE SPIRIT KNOWS
THE DEPTHS OF GOD

Proverbs 8:22-31

The Lord created me at the beginning of his work,
   the first of his acts of old.
Ages ago I was set up,
   at the first, before the beginning of the earth.
When there were no depths I was brought forth,
   when there were no springs abounding with water.
Before the mountains had been shaped,
   before the hills, I was brought forth;
before he had made the earth with its fields,
   or the first of the dust of the world.
When he established the heavens, I was there,
   when he drew a circle on the face of the deep,
when he made firm the skies above,
   when he established the fountains of the deep,
when he assigned to the sea its limit,
   so that the waters might not transgress his command,
when he marked out the foundations of the earth,
   then I was beside him, like a master workman;
and I was daily his delight,
   rejoicing before him always,
rejoicing in his inhabited world
   and delighting in the sons of men.

Yet among the mature we do impart wisdom, although it is not a wisdom of this age or of the rulers of this age, who are doomed to pass away. But we impart a secret and hidden wisdom of God, which God decreed before the ages for our glorification. None of the rulers of this age understood this; for if they had, they would have not crucified the Lord of glory. But, as it is written,

"What no eye has seen, nor ear heard,
nor the heart of man conceived,
what God has prepared for those who love him,"

God has revealed to us through the Spirit. For the Spirit searches everything, even the depths of God. For what person knows a man's thoughts except the spirit of the man which is in him? So also no one comprehends the thoughts of God except the Spirit of God. Now we have received not the spirit of the world, but the Spirit which is from God, that we might understand the gifts bestowed on us by God. And we impart this in words not taught by human wisdom but taught by the Spirit, interpreting spiritual truths to those who possess the Spirit.

Reflection

Paul has been contrasting the foolish wisdom of the world with the true but paradoxical wisdom of God which is revealed to us. The tiny, undistinguished, lower class minority which made up the earliest Church were indeed in a paradoxical situation. The Jews were anyway more or less rejected by the communities in which they lived, and the Christians were a sect of the Jews rejected by the Jews themselves; one understands why Paul could say 'we have become as the refuse of the world, the offscouring of all things' (1 Cor. 4:13). And yet they realized also the immense privilege of at last attaining to a revelation which had been hidden from so many and granted to so few. Especially at that time everyone was seeking for a way of privileged access to God or gods, by means of the many mystery religions and initiations into secret cults which were practised. And yet to the Christians alone was granted this privilege. During the ages of faith this sense of exceptional privilege was lost because little was known beyond the boundaries of the Church, but, with the expansion of our horizons geographically and chronologically, and with the contraction of Christianity, we can again appreciate it.

How great is the intimacy appears from the role of the Spirit. We understand the mystery only because we possess the Spirit, which gives us a certain co-naturality with God. Wisdom, as the Old Testament passage shows, is naturally with God, though also 'delighting in the sons of men'. It is because the Spirit searches even the depths of God that it can bring us the knowledge, and this it does by establishing a chain of co-naturality. The Spirit of God shares the divine nature, and we are brought to the knowledge of God by sharing in the Spirit.

As yet, one must not deny, our knowledge of God is rudimentary; Paul can also say that we see through a glass darkly, but there is a glimmer of light already. There is a difference between the knowledge of a Christian and that of the atheistic researcher into religious phenomena, even though his philosophical knowledge may be far more exact and higher. It would be hard to define this difference, but somehow it is a matter of life. This difference is the co-naturality of the Spirit.

18

THE HOPE OF CREATION

Isaiah 55:10-13

For as the rain and the snow come down from heaven,
    and return not thither but water the earth,
making it bring forth and sprout,
    giving seed to the sower and bread to the eater,
so shall my word be that goes forth from my mouth;
    it shall not return to me empty,
but it shall accomplish that which I purpose,
    and prosper in the things for which I sent it.
For you shall go out in joy,
    and be led forth in peace;
the mountains and the hills before you
    shall break forth into singing,
    and all the trees of the field shall clap their hands.
Instead of the thorn shall come up the cypress;
    instead of the brier shall come up the myrtle;
and it shall be to the Lord for a memorial,
    for an everlasting sign which shall not be cut off.

Romans 8:18-27

I consider that the sufferings of this present time are not
worth comparing with the glory that is to be revealed
to us. For the creation waits with eager longing for the

revealing of the sons of God; for the creation was subjected to futility, not of its own will but by the will of him who subjected it in hope; because the creation itself will be set free from its bondage to decay and obtain the glorious liberty of the children of God. We know that the whole creation has been groaning in travail together until now; and not only the creation, but we ourselves, who have the first fruits of the Spirit, groan inwardly as we wait for adoption as sons, the redemption of our bodies. For in this hope we were saved. Now hope that is seen is not hope. For who hopes for what he sees? But if we hope for what we do not see, we wait for it with patience.

Likewise the Spirit helps us in our weakness; for we do not know how to pray as we ought, but the Spirit himself intercedes for us with sighs too deep for words. And he who searches the hearts of men knows what is the mind of the Spirit, because the Spirit intercedes for the saints according to the will of God.

Reflection

Creation is in expectation, so we can never rest content with the present situation, or think that it is sufficient in itself. This gives a dynamic, progressive view of the whole of creation. At the centre of this longing to come to freedom and rebirth are the sons of God: in one way we have already reached rebirth, since we already have the beginnings of the Spirit, the pledge or first instalment which makes sense only because it is the presage of more (that is the meaning of Paul's word translated here 'first fruits'). And yet our redemption is not complete and has still to spread to the whole of our beings. There are not degrees of adoption of sons, and we are already sons through the pledge of the Spirit; but this divine sonship, or the regime of the Spirit, has not yet become so all-embracing as to suffuse our whole being — as we know only too well from the experience of our daily lives. Yet there is the certainty, guaranteed already by Isaiah, that God's work does not remain incomplete: his word does not return to him empty, but transforms even material creation.

It is within this context that Paul speaks of the Spirit's 'sighs too deep for words'. Commonly this is referred to prayer, and this of course is correct: we do not need words or any explicit prayer at all, for the very fact of being sons of God by the Spirit gives us the co-naturality with God which enables us simply to rest in God when we give ourselves to prayer. When in prayer we remove the checks and restrictions on the Spirit, the Spirit himself within us is free to work. Within a close family there is no need for words. But the meaning is wider simply than prayer. It covers our whole inadequacy: 'he who searches the hearts of men knows what is the mind of the Spirit' means that when we fail to live up to our propositions as sons of God he sees not our failure so much as the desire of the Spirit, which is nevertheless our desire, to be set free and arrive with all creation at the full stature of sons of God.

19

THE SPIRIT IN THE BIRTH OF JESUS

Luke 1:26-35

In the sixth month the angel Gabriel was sent from
God to a city of Galilee named Nazareth, to a virgin
betrothed to a man whose name was Joseph, of the
house of David; and the virgin's name was Mary. And
he came to her and said, "Hail, full of grace, the Lord
is with you!" But she was greatly troubled at the saying,
and considered in her mind what sort of greeting this
might be. And the angel said to her, "Do not be afraid,
Mary, for you have found favour with God. And behold,
you will conceive in your womb and bear a son, and you
shall call his name Jesus.

He will be great, and will be called the Son of the
    Most High;
and the Lord God will give to him the throne of his
    father David,
and he will reign over the house of Jacob for ever;
and of his kingdom there will be no end."

And Mary said to the angel, "How can this be, since
I have no husband?" And the angel said to her, "The
Holy Spirit will come upon you, and the power of
the Most High will overshadow you; therefore the child
to be born will be called holy, the Son of God.

Now the birth of Jesus Christ took place in this way. When his mother Mary had been betrothed to Joseph, before they came together she was found to be with child of the Holy Spirit; and her husband Joseph, being a just man and unwilling to put her to shame, resolved to send her away quietly. But as he considered this, behold, an angel of the Lord appeared to him in a dream, saying, "Joseph, son of David, do not fear to take Mary your wife, for that which is conceived in her is of the Holy Spirit; she will bear a son, and you shall call his name Jesus, for he will save his people from their sins."

Reflection

In the conception of Jesus the holy Spirit overshadows Mary, as the cloud representing God had overshadowed the ark of the covenant in the Old Testament, and later the temple, in both cases showing forth the presence of God. Thus simply by this expression it is suggested that Mary takes the place of the ark and the temple, that the Spirit which departed from the temple at the exile, as Ezekiel saw in his vision, returns to take its place in her. This is reinforced by the angel's greeting to her in Luke 'Hail, highly favoured (or full of grace), the Lord is with you'. The first word is not the common greeting used among the Jews, 'Peace', but is found only very rarely in the Bible, each time addressed to the daughter of Sion (the poetic personification of the chosen people) and linked to a promise of the coming of the Messiah to her. 'The Lord is with you' is an obvious indication of the presence of God. But perhaps the richest in meaning is 'highly favoured one'; it indicates a unique position, for it is a greeting made to no other. The favour is the favour of God, who has come to her and made her just as he would have her to be; his favour is an act of pure generosity and love, and yet Mary must have responded to this love. God's favour is something active and effective, not a mere good will towards someone but capable of making the subject of his favour worthy of it. Thus when it is promised that the holy Spirit will come upon her so that she may conceive the son of God, her special relationship of unparalleled favour from God has already given her a special part with the Spirit of God. The Fathers of the Church stressed the fact that she conceived in her spirit before she conceived in her womb, meaning that she was already prepared by her unique spiritual state to conceive.

The holy Spirit, here described as the power of the Most High, is the active and creative power of God. It is fitting, therefore, that the supreme act of creation, by which creation received its crown, should be ascribed to the Spirit.

F

20

THE GIFTS OF THE SPIRIT

Isaiah 11:1-9

There shall come forth a shoot from the stump of Jesse,
    and a branch shall grow out of his roots.
And the Spirit of the Lord shall rest upon him,
    the spirit of wisdom and understanding,
    the spirit of counsel and might,
    the spirit of knowledge and the fear of the Lord.
And his delight shall be in the fear of the Lord.
He shall not judge by what his eyes see,
    or decide by what his ears hear;
but with righteousness he shall judge the poor,
    and decide with enquity for the meek of the earth;
and he shall smite the earth with the rod of his mouth,
    and with the breath of his lips he shall slay
        the wicked.
Righteousness shall be the girdle of his waist,
    and faithfulness the girdle of his loins.
The wolf shall dwell with the lamb,
    and the leopard shall lie down with the kid,
and the calf and the lion and the fatling together,
    and a little child shall lead them.
The cow and the bear shall feed;
    their young shall lie down together;
    and the lion shall eat straw like the ox.

The sucking child shall play over the hole of the asp,
  and the weaned child shall put his hand on the
    adder's den.
They shall not hurt or destroy
  in all my holy mountain;
for the earth shall be full of the knowledge of the Lord
  as the waters cover the sea.

Isaiah 32:15-20

. . . until the Spirit is poured upon us from on high,
  and the wilderness becomes a fruitful field,
  and the fruitful field is deemed a forest.
Then justice will dwell in the wilderness,
  and righteousness abide in the fruitful field.
And the effect of righteousness will be peace,
  and the result of righteousness,
    quietness and trust for ever.
My people will abide in a peaceful habitation,
  in secure dwellings, and in quiet resting places.
And the forest will utterly go down,
  and the city will be utterly laid low.
Happy are you who sow beside all waters,
  who let the feet of the ox and the ass range free.

Reflection

Tradition in the Church speaks of a definite number of
gifts of the Spirit, basing its teaching a little mechanically
on Isaiah 11. In fact, of course, in this passage the gifts
of the Spirit are promised only to the coming Messiah.
But the other passage from Isaiah which we are considering shows that the Christian instinct was correct;
the Spirit which comes upon the Messiah is to spread to

all men, making a kingdom of peace and justice universal. The thing about sin is that its effect spreads: if I cheat or steal or am interested only in my own welfare, my neighbour tends to do the same, so that if the Spirit of the Messiah is to have its full effect it must consist not merely in judging between offending and offended parties, but in spreading peace to all — a peace that is symbolized by the peace in nature, the wolf dwelling with the lamb, and the leopard with the kid. From our own experience, indeed, we know that, as sin contaminates others and leads them into sin, so the man of peace and of the Spirit brings peace to those with whom he comes in contact.

One of the difficulties in considering the gifts of the Spirit is that one is left in doubt whether one is speaking of the Spirit of God or of the spirit of the man who receives these powers. This is because at the moment of revelation when these passages were written, Israel was not yet conscious that the Spirit of God was a person, and thought more of a power of God active in the world and given to man as his own, to work with. None of this need be rejected when we realize that this Power is a person; but it shows the wonderful interpenetration of the Spirit with our spirit. We are truly given the Spirit of God in such a way that we act in its strength — the actions truly being ours.

The gifts fall into pairs. The first pair concerns judgment of a situation. Wisdom is an all-embracing term, used in the Old Testament for every kind of judgment leading to right action, and — by contrast to the wisdom-doctrines of Israel's powerful neighbours — always the gift of God. But here, allied with understanding, it is perhaps more especially like the wisdom of Solomon, an ability to weigh up and penetrate a situation, that clear insight which sees immediately what is important. The next pair concerns the ability to put into practice what has been understood, either by advice and knowledge how to set about it, or by actual power to put it through. So far the gifts of the Spirit could simply be a businessman's shrewdness, and indeed the spiritual man is effective in what he sets out to do; he is the man to whom one goes for advice and to whom one lays bare one's problems because he will see to the heart of the matter and, hopefully, bring a solution. But the last pair brings the whole series firmly back to the Lord: knowledge and fear (or reverence) of the Lord are the true appreciation of what God is and so of his demands of us. In knowing God we know what it means to live as his people, for there must be a conformity of spirit: 'Be holy as I am holy'.

21

THE LIVING WATER OF THE SPIRIT

Ezekiel 47:1-12

Then he brought me back to the door of the temple:
and behold, water was issuing from below the threshold
of the temple toward the east (for the temple faced
east); and the water was flowing down from below the
south end of the threshold of the temple, south of the
altar. Then he brought me out by way of the north gate,
and led me round on the outside to the outer gate, that
faces toward the east; and the water was coming out on
the south side.

Going on eastward with a line in his hand, the man
measured a thousand cubits, and then led me through
the water; and it was ankle-deep. Again he measured a
thousand, and led me through the water; and it was
knee-deep. Again he measured a thousand, and led me
through the water; and it was up to the loins. Again
he measured a thousand, and it was a river that I could
not pass through, for the water had risen; it was deep
enough to swim in, a river that could not be passed
through. And he said to me, "Son of man, have you
seen this?"

Then he led me back along the bank of the river.
As I went back, I saw upon the bank of the river very
many trees on the one side and on the other. And he

said to me, "This water flows toward the eastern region and goes down into the Arabah; and when it enters the stagnant waters of the sea, the water will become fresh. And wherever the river goes every living creature which swarms will live, and there will be very many fish; for this water goes there, that the waters of the sea may become fresh; so everything will live where the river goes. Firshermen will stand beside the sea; from Engedi to Eneglaim it will be a place for the spreading of nets; its fish will be of very many kinds, like the fish of the Great Sea. But its swamps and marshes will not become fresh; they are to be left for salt. And on the banks, on both sides of the river, there will grow all kinds of trees for food. Their leaves will not wither nor their fruit fail, but they will bear fresh fruit every month, because the water for them flows from the sanctuary. Their fruit will be for food, and their leaves for healing."

Zechariah 14:6-9

On that day there shall be neither cold not frost. And there shall be continuous day (it is known to the Lord), not day and not night, for at evening time there shall be light.

On that day living waters shall flow out from Jerusalem, half of them to the eastern sea and half of them to the western sea; it shall continue in summer as in winter.

And the Lord will become king over all the earth; on that day the Lord will be one and his name one.

John 7:37-40

On the last day of the feast, the great day, Jesus stood up and proclaimed, "If any one thirst, let him come to me. Let him drink who believes in me. As the scripture has said, 'Out of his heart shall flow rivers of living water.'" Now this he said about the Spirit, which those who believed in him were to receive; for as yet the Spirit had not been given, because Jesus was not yet glorified.

When they heard these words, some of the people said, "This is really the prophet."

Reflection

The feast of Tabernacles, on the last day of which Jesus gave this invitation, included the ceremonies of praying for the autumn rains, in which water was brought from the main spring of Jerusalem to the temple. In the parched land of Palestine rain is vitally important, and water is almost the most important source of life. Hence in the two passages from the prophets Ezekiel and Zechariah abundance of water is one of the chief signs of the prosperity and plenty expected in the last days.

Jesus, however, takes the occasion of this feast to show that he himself is the true source of life; it is in him that true living water is to be found. They thought, following the Old Testament, that the temple would be the source of the water because God's presence was in the temple. But, as Jesus taught at his first Passover in Jerusalem (John 2:19), he himself is the true temple, for in him is given God's lasting and final presence in the world. Hence it is from him that the living water flows to the world, the living water which the evangelist tells us is the Spirit.

The symbolism of the Spirit as living water or the water of life (the expression contains both ideas) is a very rich one, and brings together many of the themes about the Spirit. The natural symbolism of water in a parched land on the edges of the desert is clear enough; the thrill of both Ezekiel and Zechariah at the luxuriant green and fertility which it brings cannot be missed. But especially life is a major theme in St John. Jesus came that we might have life, and have it more abundantly. Those who believe in him have already passed over from death to life. This life is eternal, and consists in knowing God and Jesus Christ whom he sent. Here he tells us that this life is the Spirit, the Spirit of understanding and truth which comes from him in a living stream, bringing Christians to the fullness of knowledge, and so ultimately to the full knowledge of God, and to eternal life.

SCRIPTURE FOR MEDITATION

A series of paperbacks designed to present the fruits of recent Scriptural research in a form useful for private meditation, preaching and teaching.

1. THE INFANCY NARRATIVES

The infancy narratives of Luke and Matthew are taken and studied section by section. The reader will be able to see clearly what the evangelists had in mind and to catch easily the inspiration which they wished to impart.

2. PHILIPPIANS

By comparing the epistle section by section with relevant passages of the Gospel, the author demonstrates the continuity of Paul's preaching with the teaching of Christ during his ministry. The 'reflections' add up to a complete commentary on the epistle.

3. OUR DIVINE MASTER

This is a compact synthesis of the teaching of Christ on personal relationships: God and man, ruler and subject, Jew and Gentile, rich and poor, man and wife, parents and children, etc. The conclusion which emerges is that Jesus taught what are the full demands of the law of charity in each of these relationships.

4. COLOSSIANS

This book sets forth in simple language some of the treasures contained in the apostle's splendid but difficult epistle to the Colossians. Many readers will find this more instructive than a verse-by-verse commentary.

5. CHRISTIAN DEUTERONOMY

This brilliant work of popularization elaborates the theory that the narratives collected in the central section of St Luke's gospel are arranged to match, one by one, the narratives and laws collected in the book of Deuteronomy. The author takes the passages in pairs, one from Deuteronomy and one from Luke, shows the connection between them in his 'reflection' and adds an appropriate prayer.

6. FAITH AND REVELATION

The passages of Scripture selected for this book are used as starting points for a series of reflections on the life of faith as man's response to divine revelation in nature, in the Old Testament, and in the life, death and resurrection of Christ.

7. THE PASSION

The story of the Passion is seen here in the light of Old Testament themes and prophecies and linked by a commentary sensitive alike to biblical perspectives and the enduring realities of human life.

8. THE RESURRECTION

Following St Paul as the source to which every aspect of his theology returns, the author offers reflections on the encounters of the disciples with the risen Christ.

9. THE HOLY SPIRIT

The Holy Spirit is for all Christians the source of life and power to action. Using texts of the Old and New Testament Dom Wansbrough gradually unfolds the full richness of the teaching on the Holy Spirit, from the first tentative gropings towards the understanding of the Spirit of God in the Old Testament to the full revelation of the Spirit who is a Divine Person — the Spirit of Jesus given by the Father and dwelling in the Christian. The reflections provided in this book will easily lead the reader directly into prayer.

10. THE INCARNATION

Reflections on selected biblical passages (in preparation).

Titles 1 - 6 are by John Bligh SJ.
Titles 7-10 are by Henry Wansbrough OSB.